United States
Department of
Agriculture

Forest Service

Southern
Research Station

Resource Bulletin
SRS–181

Mississippi's Timber Industry—An Assessment of Timber Product Output and Use, 2009

James W. Bentley and
Tony G. Johnson

The Authors:

James W. Bentley, Forester, U.S. Forest Service, Southern Research Station, Knoxville, TN 37919; **Tony G. Johnson**, Forester, U.S. Forest Service, Southern Research Station, Asheville, NC 28804.

July 2011

Southern Research Station
200 W.T. Weaver Blvd.
Asheville, NC 28804

Foreword

This report contains the findings of a 2009 canvass of primary wood-using plants in Mississippi, and presents changes in product output and residue use since 2007. It complements the Forest Inventory and Analysis periodic inventory of volume and removals from the State's timberland. The canvass was conducted to determine the amount and source of wood receipts and annual timber product drain, by county, in 2009 and to determine interstate and cross-regional movement of industrial roundwood. Only primary wood-using mills were canvassed. Primary mills are those that process roundwood in log or bolt form or as chipped roundwood. Examples of industrial roundwood products are saw logs, pulpwood, veneer logs, poles, and logs used for composite board products. Mills producing products from residues generated at primary and secondary processors were not canvassed. Trees chipped in the woods were included in the estimate of timber drain only if they were delivered to a primary domestic manufacturer.

A canvass of all wood processors in Mississippi was conducted in 2010 to obtain information for 2009. In addition, roundwood from out-of-State mills known to be using logs or bolts harvested from Mississippi timberland was incorporated into Mississippi production estimates. Each mill was canvassed by mail or through personal contact at plant locations. Telephone contacts followed mailed questionnaire responses when additional information or clarification of a response was necessary. In the event of a nonresponse, data collected in previous surveys were updated using current data collected for mills of similar size, product type, and location. Surveys for all timber products other than pulpwood began in 1948, and are currently conducted every 2 years.

Pulpwood production data were taken from an annual canvass of all southern pulpmills. Medium density fiberboard, insulating board, and hardboard plants were included in this survey.

Acknowledgments

The Southern Research Station (SRS) gratefully acknowledges the cooperation and assistance provided by the Mississippi Forestry Commission, Brian Wharton, and the FIA field crew, in collecting mill data. Appreciation is also extended to forest industry and mill managers for providing timber products information.

The authors thank Richard Bohnen and Brian Wharton for review and comments; Carolyn Steppleton and Michael Howell for their tireless efforts in processing and accuracy of the data; Helen Beresford for timber product output database maintenance and support; Anne Jenkins, Janet Griffin, Sharon Johnson, and Charlene Walker for tables, graphs, statistical checking, and styling; and the SRS Technical Publications Team for editorial review and publication of this report.

Timber Product Output Database Retrieval System

The Forest Inventory and Analysis (FIA) Research Work Unit of the USDA Forest Service developed the Timber Product Output (TPO) Database Retrieval System to help customers answer questions about timber harvesting and use in the Southern region. This system acts as an interface to a standard set of consistently coded TPO data for each State and county in the region and Nation. This regional and national set of TPO data consists of 11 variables that describe for each county the roundwood products harvested, logging residues left in the woods, other timber removals (i.e. land clearing and reserved timber removals), and wood and bark residues generated by the county's primary wood-using mills. The system is available through the FIA Web site: http://srsfia2.fs.fed.us/.

The database is well documented and easy to use. The retrieval system allows the user to select the TPO variables of interest and generate a standard set of timber products, removals, and mill residue tables for the specified resource area, State, or region. The system has been logically divided into two sections to assist the user in making specific data requests. In section 1, the user is asked to define the resource area, and section 2 generates tables for the specified area. In each section, the user is asked to select specific options that will serve to customize the database retrieval.

There are four options available for defining the geographic area of interest. Each option provides an increasing level of detail. The region, subregion, State, or county defines an area. The user selects the option that best suits the level of detail required. Users who select county as an option should be aware that some counties have been combined due to data sensitivity. These combined counties are identified with asterisks in the output tables.

The TPO contacts are listed to provide additional explanation or clarification.

Tony Johnson
Southern Research Station
USDA Forest Service
200 W.T. Weaver Blvd.
Asheville, NC 28804
tjohnson09@fs.fed.us
828-257-4888

Helen Beresford
Southern Research Station
USDA Forest Service
4700 Old Kingston Pike
Knoxville, TN 37919
hberesford@fs.fed.us
865-862-2091

James Bentley
Southern Research Station
USDA Forest Service
4700 Old Kingston Pike
Knoxville, TN 37919
jbentley@fs.fed.us
865-862-2056

Carolyn Steppleton
Southern Research Station
USDA Forest Service
200 W.T. Weaver Blvd.
Asheville, NC 28804
csteppleton@fs.fed.us
828-257-4848

Contents

Page

Output of Industrial Timber Products 1

   All Products 1

   Saw Logs 2

   Pulpwood 3

   Veneer Logs 3

   Composite Panels 5

   Other Industrial Products 5

Plant Byproducts 5

County Data 6

Total Roundwood Output 6

   Source 6

   Ownership 7

   Species 7

References 8

Glossary 9

Conversion Factors 12

Species List 13

Appendix 15

   Index of Tables 17

   Tables A.1–A.18[a] 19

[a] All tables in this report are available in Microsoft® Excel workbook files. Upon request, these files will be supplied in the format the customer requests. The use of trade or firm names in this publication is for reader information and does not imply endorsement by the U.S. Department of Agriculture of any product or service.

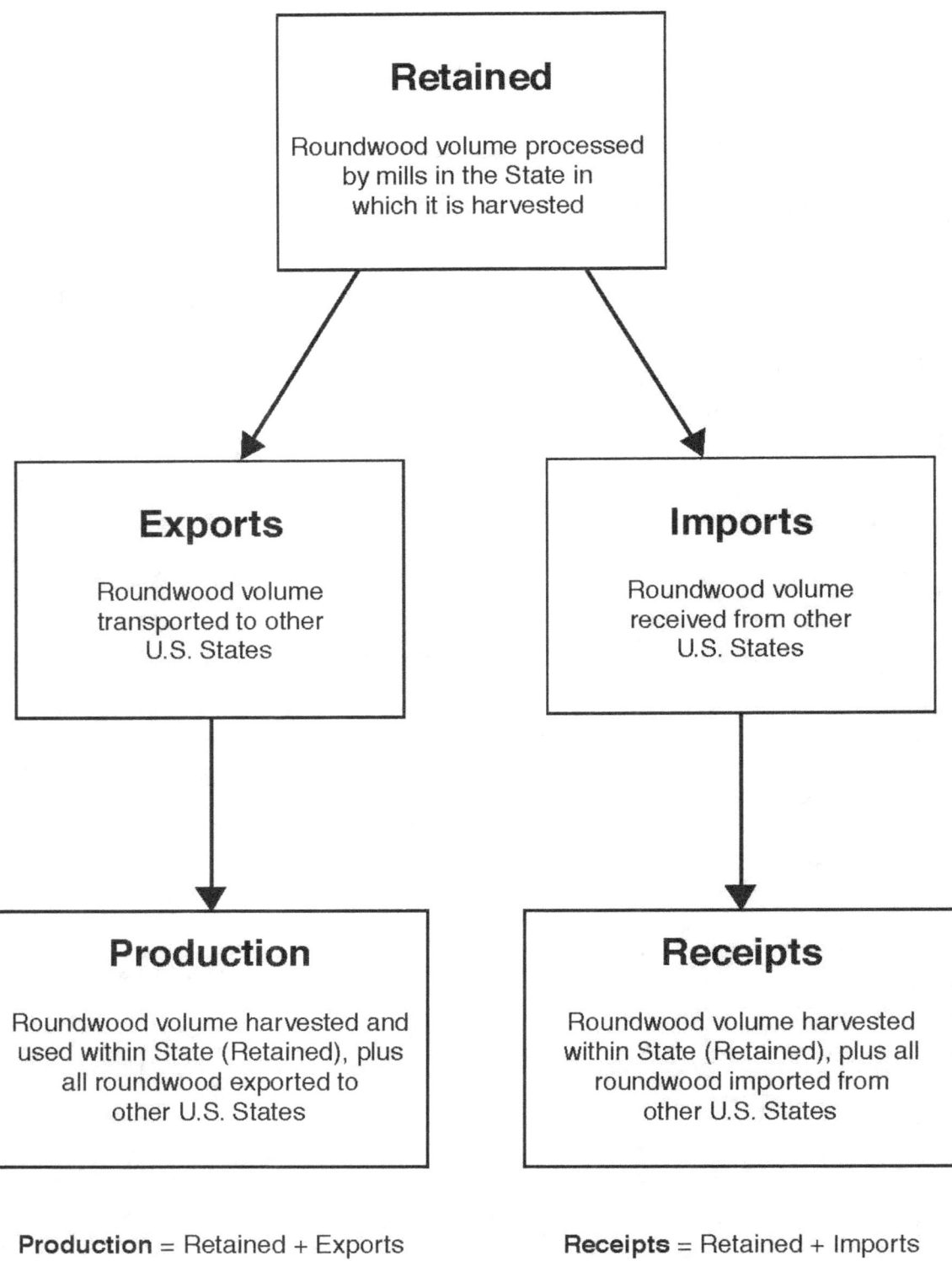

Figure 1—Movement of roundwood exports and imports within the United States.

Mississippi's Timber Industry—An Assessment of Timber Product Output and Use, 2009

James W. Bentley and Tony G. Johnson

Output of Industrial Timber Products

Note: Certain terms used in this report—retained, export, import, production, and receipts—have specialized meanings and relationships unique to the Forest Inventory and Analysis Units across the country that deal with timber product output (TPO) (fig. 1). Unless otherwise indicated, the context for production and receipts comparisons (increases, decreases, or stabilizations) throughout the report is the change from 2007 to 2009.

All Products

- TPO from roundwood was down 209.1 million cubic feet, or 23 percent, to 685.0 million cubic feet.

- Output of softwood roundwood products decreased 22 percent, totaling 529.4 million cubic feet, while output of hardwood roundwood products was down 27 percent to 155.6 million cubic feet (fig. 2).

- Pulpwood and saw logs were the principal roundwood products in 2009. Combined output of these two products totaled 616.0 million cubic feet and accounted for 90 percent of the State's total industrial roundwood output (fig. 3).

- Total receipts at Mississippi mills, which included roundwood harvested and retained in the State and roundwood imported from other States, decreased 30 percent to 520.3 million cubic feet, while output of utilized plant byproducts declined 130.4 million cubic feet to 185.8 million cubic feet.

- The number of primary roundwood-using plants in 2009 for Mississippi was 73, a loss of 11 mills from 2007 (fig. 4).

- Across all products, 69 percent of roundwood harvested was retained for processing at Mississippi mills. Exports of roundwood to other States amounted to 214.9 million cubic feet, while imports of roundwood amounted to 50.1 million cubic feet, making the State a net exporter

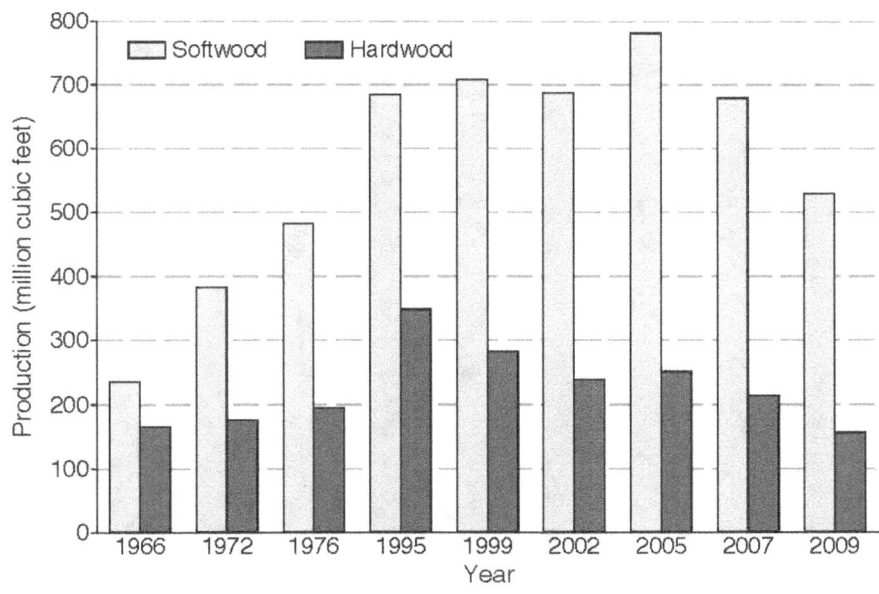

Figure 2—Roundwood production for all products by species group and year, (see page 8 for references for individual years) Mississippi.

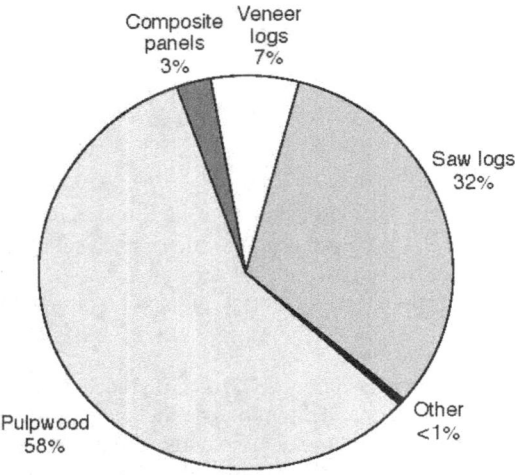

Total 685 million cubic feet

Figure 3—Roundwood production by type of product, Mississippi, 2009.

of roundwood. Tables A.8 to A.11 show exports to and imports from other States by individual product type.

Saw Logs

- Saw logs accounted for 32 percent of the State's total roundwood products. Output of softwood saw logs decreased 45 percent to 165.0 million cubic feet (902 million board feet, International ¼-inch rule), while that of hardwood saw logs decreased 30 percent to 54.5 million cubic feet (325 million board feet, International ¼-inch rule) (fig. 5).

- In 2009, Mississippi had 57 sawmills, a loss of 9 mills since 2007. The total number of sawmills does not include the several one-person sawmills in the State. Total saw-log receipts were down 169.6 million cubic feet to 215.3 million cubic feet. Softwood saw-log receipts decreased 47 percent to 162.1 million cubic feet, while those of hardwoods decreased 31 percent to 53.2 million cubic feet. Of the operating mills in 2009, 21 percent had

Figure 4—Primary wood-using mills by region, Mississippi, 2009.

2

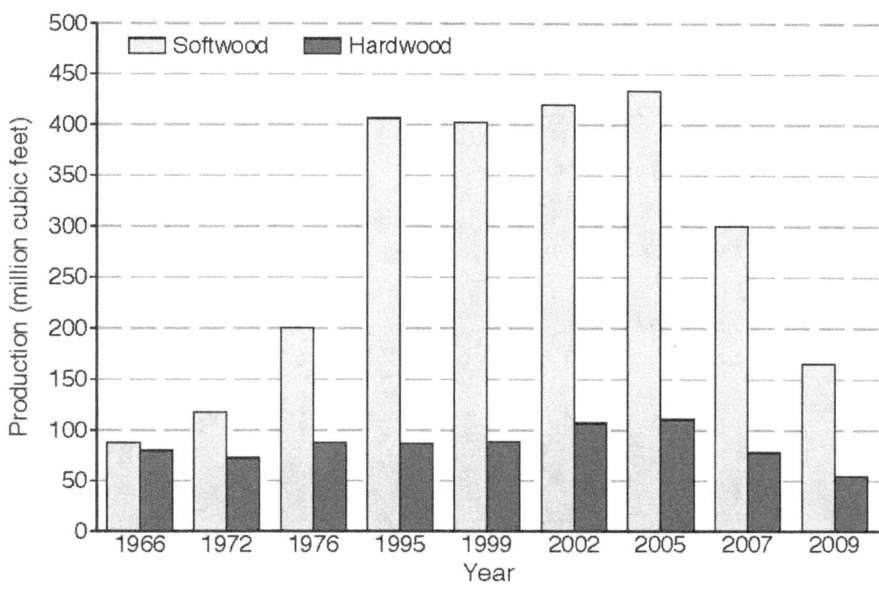

Figure 5— Roundwood saw-log production by species group and year, (see page 8 for references for individual years) Mississippi.

receipts of < 5 million board feet, while 56 percent had receipts > 10 million board feet. Those 32 mills, however, accounted for 90 percent of total saw-log receipts.

* Mississippi retained 86 percent of its saw-log production for in-State manufacture, with saw-log exports exceeding imports by 4.3 million cubic feet in 2009.

Pulpwood

* Total pulpwood production, including chipped round-wood, was down 1 percent to 396.4 million cubic feet and accounted for 58 percent of the State's total round-wood TPO. Softwood output increased 9 percent to 298.5 million cubic feet (4.11 million cords); hardwood output decreased 23 percent to 97.9 million cubic feet (1.31 million cords) (fig. 6).

* Five pulpmill facilities were operating and receiving roundwood in Mississippi in 2009, the same as in 2007. Total pulpwood receipts for these mills decreased 4.8 million cubic feet to 232.7 million cubic feet, accounting for 45 percent of total receipts for all mills.

* Fifty-four percent of roundwood cut for pulpwood was retained for processing at Mississippi pulpmills. Round-wood pulpwood accounted for 84 percent of total known

exports and 35 percent of total imports. Roundwood pulpwood exports amounted to 181.5 million cubic feet, and imports amounted to 17.7 million cubic feet, making the State a net exporter of roundwood pulpwood.

Veneer Logs

* Output of veneer logs in 2009 totaled 46.9 million cubic feet and accounted for 7 percent of the State's total round-wood TPO volume. Softwood veneer production was down 37 percent to 44.5 million cubic feet (260 million board feet, International ¼-inch rule); output of hardwood veneer logs decreased 51 percent to 2.4 million cubic feet (15 million board feet, International ¼-inch rule) (fig. 7).

* The number of veneer mills operating in Mississippi for 2009 was seven, a loss of one mill since 2007. Receipts of veneer logs decreased 40 percent to 50.4 million cubic feet.

* Mississippi retained 97 percent of its veneer-log produc-tion for processing at in-State veneer mills. Imports amounted to 4.9 million cubic feet, and exports totaled 1.4 million cubic feet, making the State a net importer of roundwood veneer logs.

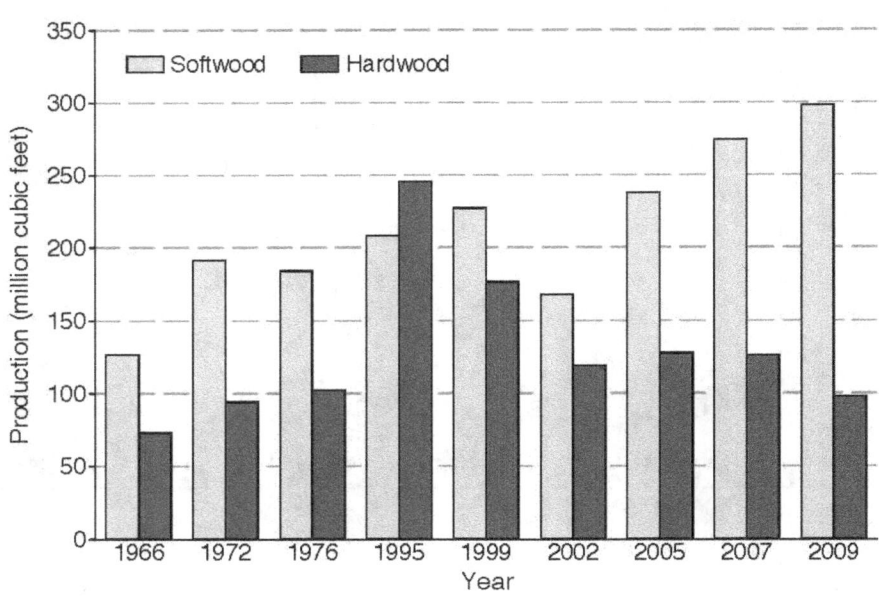

Figure 6—Roundwood pulpwood production by species group and year, (see page 8 for references for individual years) Mississippi.

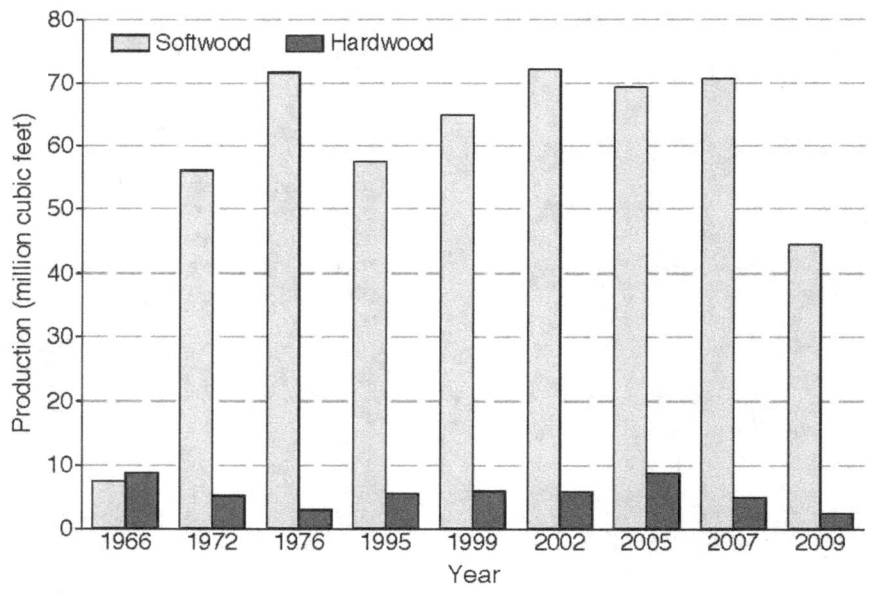

Figure 7—Roundwood veneer-log production by species group and year, (see page 8 for references for individual years) Mississippi.

Composite Panels

- Roundwood harvested from Mississippi's forests for composite panels decreased 51 percent and totaled 18.5 million cubic feet. Softwood output was down 46 percent to 18.0 million cubic feet (248,000 cords); hardwood production was down 89 percent to 526,000 cubic feet (7,000 cords) (fig. 8). Softwood output accounted for 97 percent of all composite panel production in Mississippi.

Other Industrial Products

- Roundwood harvested for other industrial uses such as poles, posts, mulch, firewood, logs for log homes, industrial fuel, and all other industrial products totaled 3.6 million cubic feet, a 137 percent increase from 2007. Softwood made-up all of the other industrial products volume.

- Receipts of other industrial mills such as poles, posts, mulch, firewood, logs for log homes, industrial fuel, composite panels and all other industrial products decreased 45 percent to 21.8 million cubic feet. Industrial fuel accounted for 10 percent or 2.2 million cubic feet of these receipts.

Plant Byproducts

- In 2009, processing of primary products in Mississippi mills generated 185.9 million cubic feet of wood and bark residues. Coarse residues from all primary products amounted to 72.4 million cubic feet, while bark volume totaled 51.0 million cubic feet. Collectively, sawdust and shavings made-up 34 percent of total residues, or 62.6 million cubic feet (fig. 9).

- The processing of saw logs generated 129.0 million cubic feet of mill residues, accounting for 69 percent of the total residues produced (fig. 10).

- Ninety-nine percent, or 185.8 million cubic feet, of the wood and bark residues were used for a product; < 1 percent of the residues were not used for a product; 57 percent of the residues were used for industrial fuel and 35 percent were used for fiber products (fig. 11). Eighty-nine percent, or 64.3 million cubic feet, of the coarse residues were used for fiber products. Most of the bark was used for industrial fuel or other miscellaneous products, while 81 percent of the sawdust and shavings were used for industrial fuel.

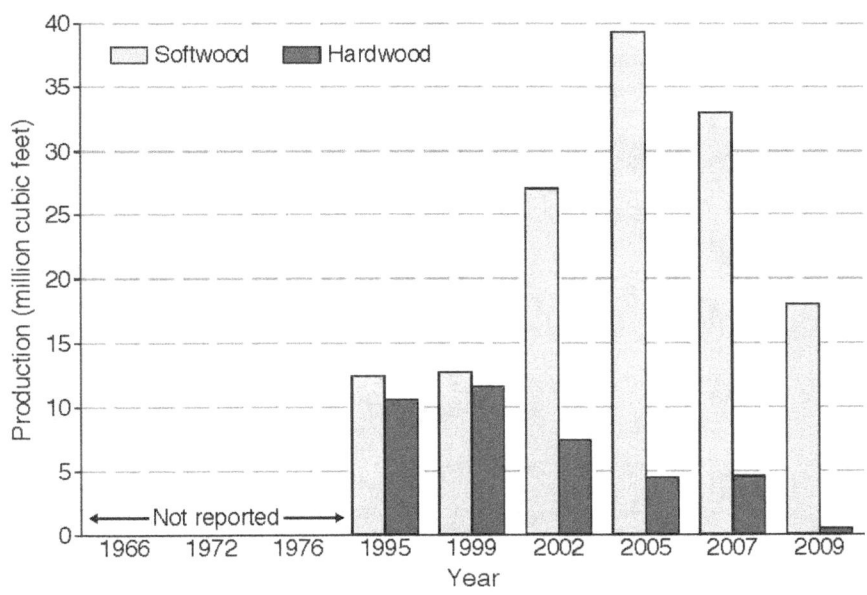

Figure 8— Roundwood production for composite panels by species group and year, (see page 8 for references for individual years) Mississippi.

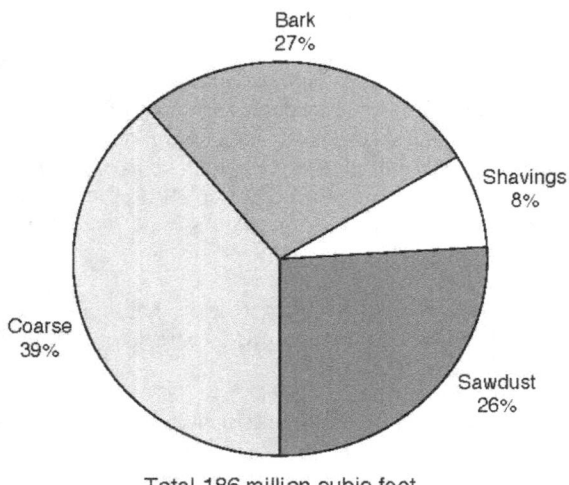

Figure 9—Primary mill residue by residue type, Mississippi, 2009.

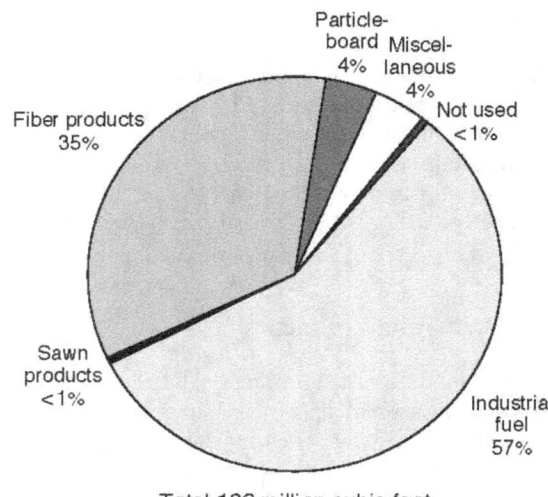

Figure 11—Disposal of residue by product, Mississippi, 2009.

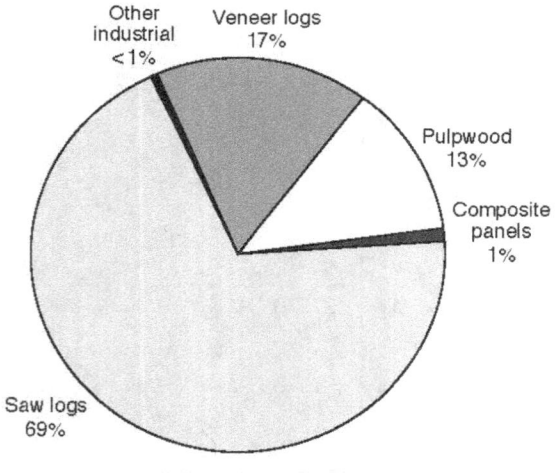

Figure 10—Primary mill residue produced by roundwood type, Mississippi, 2009.

County Data

- Table A.14 shows softwood and hardwood product output by county and individual product type. All 82 counties in Mississippi had roundwood output. Five counties (Amite, Kemper, Lauderdale, Lincoln, and Marion) had combined softwood and hardwood product output of > 20 million cubic feet each. These five counties total product output amounted to 124.5 million cubic feet and accounted for 18 percent of the State's total product output.

Total Roundwood Output

Using the most recent inventory data for Mississippi, product output by source, ownership, and detailed species group was estimated.

Source

- In addition to the 685.0 million cubic feet of roundwood output for industrial roundwood, an estimated 17.9 million cubic feet were harvested for residential fuelwood, bringing Mississippi's total roundwood output to 702.9 million cubic feet.

- Ninety-one percent of total roundwood output was considered growing-stock volume (sawtimber and poletimber) from timberland sources. Other sources (such as saplings; stumps, tops, and limbs of trees on timberland; and trees on nonforest land) contributed an estimated 63.2 million cubic feet, or 9 percent of total roundwood output (fig. 12).

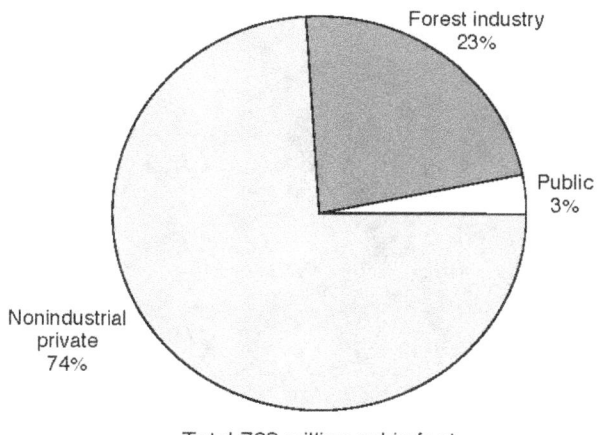

Total 703 million cubic feet

Figure 13—Roundwood output by ownership, Mississippi, 2009.

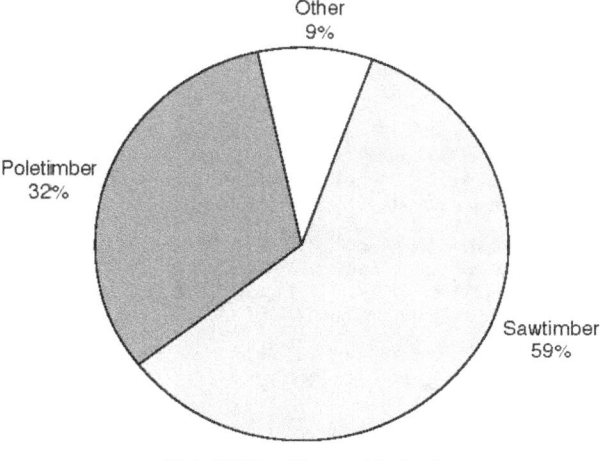

Total 703 million cubic feet

Figure 12—Roundwood output by source, Mississippi, 2009.

Species

- The loblolly and shortleaf pine group provided the most volume of any softwood species group, accounting for 86 percent of the total softwood output (fig. 14). The longleaf-slash pine type accounted for 11 percent of the softwood output. In hardwoods, the red oak and white oak groups combined accounted for 86.4 million cubic feet, or 51 percent of total hardwood output (fig. 15).

Ownership

- An estimated 519.7 million cubic feet, or 74 percent, of the total roundwood output came from nonindustrial private forest lands. Forest industry lands contributed 160.6 million cubic feet, or 23 percent of the output. Public lands made-up the remaining 3 percent, or 22.6 million cubic feet (fig. 13).

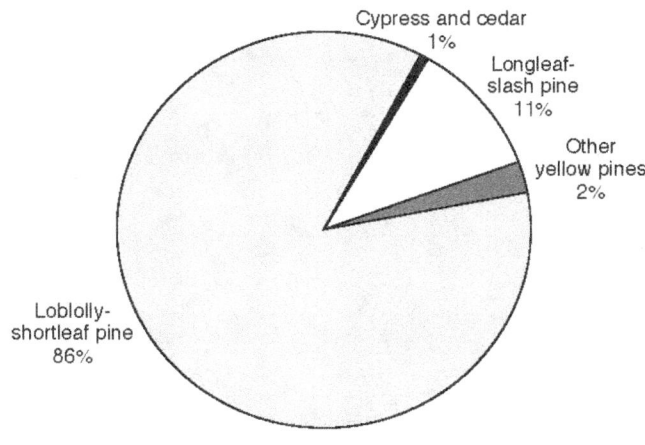

Total 533 million cubic feet

Figure 14—Roundwood output by softwood species group, Mississippi, 2009.

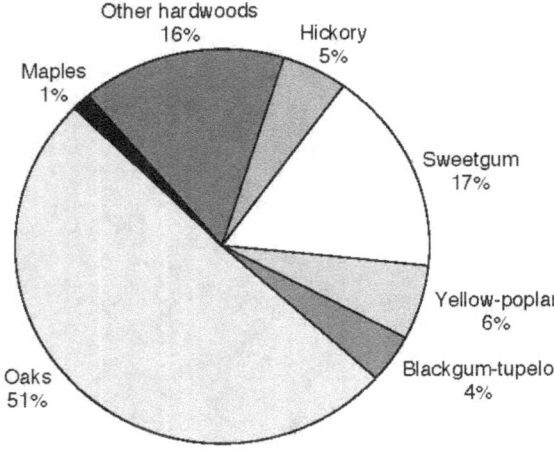

Total 170 million cubic feet

Figure 15—Roundwood output by hardwood species group, Mississippi, 2009.

References

Bentley, J.W.; Howell, M.; Johnson, T.G. 2008. Mississippi's timber industry—an assessment of timber product output and use, 2005. Resour. Bull. SRS–131. Asheville, NC: U.S. Department of Agriculture Forest Service, Southern Research Station. 32 p. [2005].

Bentley, J.W.; Johnson, T.G.; Howell, M. 2002. Mississippi's timber industry—an assessment of timber product output and use, 1999. Resour. Bull. SRS–80. Asheville, NC: U.S. Department of Agriculture Forest Service, Southern Research Station. 40 p. [1999].

Bertelson, D.F. 1973. Mississippi forest industries, 1972. Resour. Bull. SO–43. New Orleans: U.S. Department of Agriculture Forest Service, Southern Forest Experiment Station. 27 p. [1972].

Bertelson, D.F. 1978. Mississippi forest industries, 1976. Resour. Bull. SO–68. New Orleans: U.S. Department of Agriculture Forest Service, Southern Forest Experiment Station. 25 p. [1976].

Howell, M.; Johnson, T.G. 2009. Mississippi's timber industry—an assessment of timber product output and use, 2007. Resour. Bull. SRS–157. Asheville, NC: U.S. Department of Agriculture Forest Service, Southern Research Station. 31 p. [2007].

Howell, M.; Johnson, T.G.; Bentley, J.W. 2005. Mississippi's timber industry—an assessment of timber product output and use, 2002. Resour. Bull. SRS–102. Asheville, NC: U.S. Department of Agriculture Forest Service, Southern Research Station. 45 p. [2002].

Little, E.L., Jr. 1979. Checklist of United States trees (native and naturalized). Agric. Handb. 541. Washington, DC: U.S. Department of Agriculture. 375 p.

Stratton, D.P.; Howell, M.; Romedy, R. 1998. Mississippi's timber industry—an assessment of timber product output and use, 1995. Resour. Bull. SRS–29. Asheville, NC: U.S. Department of Agriculture Forest Service, Southern Research Station. 23 p. [1995].

Van Hooser, D.D. 1968. Mississippi forest industry. Resour. Bull. SO–12. New Orleans: U.S. Department of Agriculture Forest Service, Southern Forest Experiment Station. 25 p. [1966].

Glossary

Board foot. A unit of measure applied to lumber that is 1-foot long, 1-foot wide, and 1-inch thick (or its equivalent) and also associated with roundwood as to its potential yield of such products.

Byproducts. Primary wood products, e.g., pulp chips, animal bedding, and fuelwood, recycled from mill residues.

Composite panels. Roundwood products manufactured into chips, wafers, strands, flakes, shavings, or sawdust and then reconstituted into a variety of panel and engineered lumber products.

Consumption. The quantity of a commodity, such as pulpwood, utilized by a particular mill or group of mills.

Drain. The volume of roundwood removed from any geographic area where timber is grown.

Exports. The volume of domestic roundwood utilized by mills outside the State where timber was cut.

Fiber products. Byproducts used in the manufacture of pulp, paper, paperboard, and composite products, such as chipboard.

Growing-stock removals. The growing-stock volume removed from poletimber and sawtimber trees in the timberland inventory. (Note: Includes volume removed for roundwood products, logging residues, and other removals.)

Growing-stock trees. Living trees of commercial species classified as sawtimber, poletimber, saplings, and seedlings. Growing-stock trees must contain at least one 12-foot or two 8-foot logs in the saw-log portion, currently or potentially (if too small to qualify). The log(s) must meet dimension and merchantability standards and have, currently or potentially, one-third of the gross board-foot volume in sound wood.

Growing-stock volume. The cubic-foot volume of sound wood in growing-stock trees at least 5.0 inches d.b.h. from a 1-foot stump to a minimum 4.0-inch top d.o.b. of the central stem.

Hardwoods. Dicotyledonous trees, usually broadleaf and deciduous.

Soft hardwoods. Hardwood species with an average specific gravity of ≤0.50, such as gums, yellow-poplar, cottonwoods, red maple, basswoods, and willows.

Hard hardwoods. Hardwood species with an average specific gravity >0.50, such as oaks, hard maples, hickories, and beech.

Imports. The volume of domestic roundwood delivered to a mill or group of mills in a specific State but harvested outside that State.

Industrial fuelwood. A roundwood product, with or without bark, used to generate energy at a manufacturing facility such as a wood-using mill.

Industrial roundwood products. Any primary use of the main stem of a tree, such as saw logs, pulpwood, veneer logs, intended to be processed into primary wood products such as lumber, wood pulp, sheathing, at primary wood-using mills.

International ¼-inch rule. A log rule or formula for estimating the board-foot volume of logs, allowing ½-inch of taper for each 4-foot length. The rule appears in a number of forms that allow for kerf. In the form used by FIA, a ¼-inch of kerf is assumed. This rule is used as the U.S. Forest Service standard log rule in the Eastern United States.

Log. A primary forest product harvested in long, primarily 8-, 12-, and 16-foot lengths.

Logging residues. The unused portion of trees cut or destroyed during logging operations.

Merchantable portion. That portion of live trees 5.0 inches d.b.h. and larger between a 1-foot stump and a minimum 4.0-inch top d.o.b. on the central stem. That portion of primary forks from the point of occurrence to a minimum 4.0-inch top d.o.b. is included.

Merchantable volume. Solid-wood volume in the merchantable portion of live trees.

Noncommercial species. Tree species of typically small size, poor form, or inferior quality that normally do not develop into trees suitable for industrial wood products.

Nonforest land. Land that has never supported forests and land formerly forested where timber production is precluded by development for other uses.

Nongrowing-stock sources. The net volume removed from the nongrowing-stock portions of poletimber and sawtimber trees (stumps, tops, limbs, cull sections of central stem) and from any portion of a rough, rotten, sapling, dead, or nonforest tree.

Other forest land. Forest land other than timberland and productive reserved forest land. It includes available and reserved forest land that is incapable of producing annually 20 cubic feet per acre of industrial wood under natural conditions because of adverse site conditions such as sterile soils, dry climate, poor drainage, high elevation, steepness, or rockiness.

Other products. A miscellaneous category of roundwood products, e.g., cooperage, excelsior, shingles, and mill residue byproducts (charcoal, bedding, mulch, etc.).

Other removals. The growing-stock volume of trees removed from the inventory by cultural operations such as timber stand improvement, land clearing, and other changes in land use, resulting in the removal of the trees from timberland.

Other sources. (See: Nongrowing-stock sources.)

Ownership. The property owned by one ownership unit, including all parcels of land in the United States.

National forest land. Federal land that has been legally designated as national forests or purchase units, and other land under the administration of the Forest Service, including experimental areas and Bankhead-Jones Title III land.

Forest industry land. Land owned by companies or individuals operating primary wood-using plants.

Nonindustrial private forest (NIPF) land. Privately owned land excluding forest industry land.

Corporate. Owned by corporations, including incorporated farm ownerships.

Individual. All lands owned by individuals, including farm operators.

Other public. An ownership class that includes all public lands except national forests.

Miscellaneous Federal land. Federal land other than national forests.

State, county, and municipal land. Land owned by States, counties, and local public agencies or municipalities, or land leased to these governmental units for 50 years or more.

Plant residues. Wood material generated in the production of timber products at primary manufacturing plants.

Coarse residues. Material, such as slabs, edgings, trim, veneer cores and ends, which is suitable for chipping.

Fine residues. Material, such as sawdust, shavings, and veneer residue, which is not suitable for chipping.

Plant byproducts. Residues (coarse or fine) used in the further manufacture of industrial products for consumer use, or as fuel.

Unused plant residues. Residues (coarse or fine) that are not used for any product, including fuel.

Poletimber-size trees. Softwoods 5.0 to 8.9 inches d.b.h. and hardwoods 5.0 to 10.9 inches d.b.h.

Posts, poles, and pilings. Roundwood products milled (cut or peeled) into standard sizes (lengths and circumferences) to be put in the ground to provide vertical and lateral support in buildings, foundations, utility lines, and fences. May also include nonindustrial (unmilled) products.

Primary wood-using plants. Industries that convert round-wood products (saw logs, veneer logs, pulpwood, etc.) into primary wood products, such as lumber, veneer or sheathing, wood pulp.

Production. The total volume of known roundwood harvested from land within a State, regardless of where it is consumed. Production is the sum of timber harvested and used within a State, and all roundwood exported to other States.

Pulpwood. A roundwood product that will be reduced to individual wood fibers by chemical or mechanical means. The fibers are used to make a broad generic group of pulp products that includes paper products, as well as fiberboard, insulating board, and paperboard.

Receipts. The quantity or volume of industrial roundwood received at a mill or by a group of mills in a State, regardless of the geographic source. Volume of roundwood receipts is equal to the volume of roundwood retained in a State plus roundwood imported from other States.

Residential fuelwood. The volume of roundwood harvested to produce heat for residential settings.

Retained. Roundwood volume harvested from and processed by mills within the same State.

Rotten trees. Live trees of commercial species not containing at least one 12-foot saw log, or two noncontiguous saw logs, each 8 feet or longer, now or prospectively, primarily because of rot or missing sections, and with less than one-third of the gross board-foot tree volume in sound material.

Rough trees. Live trees of commercial species not containing at least one 12-foot saw log, or two noncontiguous saw logs, each 8 feet or longer, now or prospectively, primarily because of roughness, poor form, splits, and cracks, and with less than one-third of the gross board-foot tree volume in sound material; and live trees of noncommercial species.

Roundwood (roundwood logs). Logs, bolts, or other round sections cut from trees for industrial manufacture or consumer uses.

Roundwood chipped. Any timber cut primarily for industrial manufacture, delivered to nonpulpmills, chipped, and then sold to pulpmills for use as fiber. Includes tops, jump sections, whole trees, and pulpwood sticks.

Roundwood product drain. That portion of total drain used for a product.

Roundwood products. Any primary product, such as lumber, veneer, composite panels, poles, pilings, pulp, or fuelwood that is produced from roundwood.

Salvable dead trees. Standing or downed dead trees that were formerly growing stock and considered merchantable. Trees must be at least 5.0 inches d.b.h. to qualify.

Saplings. Live trees 1.0 to 5.0 inches d.b.h.

Saw log. A roundwood product, usually 8 feet in length or longer, processed into a variety of sawn products such as lumber, cants, pallets, railroad ties, and timbers.

Saw-log portion. The part of the bole of sawtimber trees between a 1-foot stump and the saw-log top.

Saw-log top. The point on the bole of sawtimber trees above which a conventional saw log cannot be produced. The minimum saw-log top is 7.0 inches d.o.b. for softwoods and 9.0 inches d.o.b. for hardwoods for FIA standards.

Sawtimber-size trees. Softwoods 9.0 inches d.b.h. and larger and hardwoods 11.0 inches d.b.h. and larger.

Sawtimber volume. Growing-stock volume in the saw-log portion of sawtimber-sized trees in board feet (International ¼-inch rule).

Seedlings. Trees < 1.0 inch d.b.h. and > 1 foot tall for hardwoods, > 6 inches tall for softwoods, and > 0.5 inch in diameter at ground level for longleaf pine.

Select red oaks. A group of several red oak species composed of cherrybark, Shumard, and northern red oaks. Other red oak species are included in the "other red oaks" group.

Select white oaks. A group of several white oak species composed of white, swamp chestnut, swamp white, chinkapin, Durand, and bur oaks. Other white oak species are included in the "other white oaks" group.

Softwoods. Coniferous trees, usually evergreen, having leaves that are needles or scale like.

Standard cord. A unit of measure applied to roundwood, usually bolts or split wood. It is a stack of wood 4 feet high, 4 feet wide, and 8 feet long encompassing 128 cubic feet of wood, bark, and air space. This usually translates to approximately 75.0 to 81.0 cubic feet of solid wood for pulpwood, because pulpwood is more uniform.

Standard unit. A unit measure applied to roundwood timber products. Board feet (International ¼-inch rule) is the standard unit used for saw logs and veneer; cords are used for pulpwood, composite panel, and fuelwood; hundred pieces for poles; thousand pieces for posts; and thousand cubic feet for all other miscellaneous forest products.

Timberland. Forest land capable of producing 20 cubic feet of industrial wood per acre per year and not withdrawn from timber utilization.

Timber product output. The total volume of roundwood products from all sources plus the volume of byproducts recovered from mill residues (equals roundwood product drain).

Timber products. Roundwood products and byproducts.

Timber removals. The total volume of trees removed from the timberland inventory by harvesting, cultural operations such as stand improvement, land clearing, or changes in land use. (Note: Includes roundwood products, logging residues, and other removals.)

Tree. Woody plants having one erect perennial stem or trunk at least 3 inches d.b.h., a more or less definitely formed crown of foliage, and a height of at least 13 feet (at maturity).

Upper-stem portion. The part of the main stem of saw-timber trees above the saw-log top and the minimum top diameter of 4.0 inches outside bark, or to the point where the main stem breaks into limbs.

Utilization studies. Studies conducted on active logging operations to develop factors for merchantable portions of trees left in the woods (logging residues), logging damage, and utilization of the unmerchantable portion of growing-stock trees and nongrowing-stock trees.

Veneer log. A roundwood product either rotary cut, sliced, stamped, or sawn into a variety of veneer products such as plywood, finished panels, veneer sheets, or sheathing.

Weight. A unit of measure for mill residues, expressed as oven-dry tons (2,000 oven-dry pounds).

Conversion Factors[a]

Saw logs	
Softwood	0.18349 cubic foot = 1 board foot
	5.45 board feet = 1 cubic foot
Hardwood	0.16807 cubic foot = 1 board foot
	5.95 board feet = 1 cubic foot
Veneer logs	
Softwood	0.17094 cubic foot = 1 board foot
	5.85 board feet = 1 cubic foot
Hardwood	0.16260 cubic foot = 1 board foot
	6.15 board feet = 1 cubic foot
Pulpwood[b]	
Softwood	72.6 cubic feet per cord
Hardwood	75.0 cubic feet per cord

[a] Conversion factors vary with stem size (d.b.h.) and species. The factors shown are for trees of average diameters removed in Mississippi during the most recent survey period.

[b] Cubic feet of solid wood per cord.

Species List[a]

Common name	Scientific name[b]	Common name	Scientific name[b]
Softwoods		**Hardwoods (continued)**	
Atlantic white-cedar	*Chamaecyparis thyoides* (L.) B.S.P.	Bigleaf magnolia	*M. macrophylla* Michx.
Southern redcedar	*Juniperus silicicola* (Small) Bailey	Sweetbay	*M. virginiana* L.
Eastern redcedar	*J. virginiana* L.	Apple	*Malus* spp. Mill.
Shortleaf pine	*Pinus echinata* Mill.	Chinaberry	*Melia azedarach* L.
Slash pine	*P. elliottii* Mill.	White mulberry	*Morus alba* L.
Spruce pine	*P. glabra* Walt.	Red mulberry	*M. rubra* L.
Longleaf pine	*P. palustris* Mill.	Water tupelo	*Nyssa aquatica* L.
Loblolly pine	*P. taeda* L.	Blackgum	*N. sylvatica* Marsh.
Virginia pine	*P. virginiana* Mill.	Swamp tupelo	*N. sylvatica* var. *biflora* (Walt.) Sarg.
Baldcypress	*Taxodium distichum* L.	Eastern hophornbeam	*Ostrya virginiana* (Mill.) K. Koch
Hardwoods		Sourwood	*Oxydendrum arboreum* L.
Florida maple	*Acer barbatum* Michx.	Royal paulownia	*Paulownia tomentosa* (Thunb.) Sieb. & Zucc. ex Steud.
Boxelder	*A. negundo* L.		
Red maple	*A. rubrum* L.	Redbay	*Persea borbonia* L.
Silver maple	*A. saccharinum* L.	Water-elm	*Planera aquatica* J. F. Gmel.
Sugar maple	*A. saccharum* Marsh.	American sycamore	*Platanus occidentalis* L.
Ohio buckeye	*Aesculus glabra* Willd.	Cottonwood	*Populus* spp. L.
Buckeye	*A.* spp. L.	Black cherry	*Prunus serotina* Ehrh.
Ailanthus	*Ailanthus altissima* Mill.	Plums, cherries (other than black cherry)	*P.* spp. L.
Tung-oil tree	*Aleurites fordii* Hemsl.		
Serviceberry	*Amelanchier* spp. Medic.	White oak	*Quercus alba* L.
River birch	*Betula nigra* L.	Scarlet oak	*Q. coccinea* Muenchh.
Chittamwood	*Bumelia* spp. (Michx.) Pers.	Durand oak	*Q. durandii* Buckl.
American hornbeam	*Carpinus caroliniana* Walt.	Southern red oak	*Q. falcata* Michx.
Hickory	*Carya* spp. Nutt.	Cherrybark oak	*Q. falcata* var. *pagodifolia* Ell.
Water hickory	*C. aquatica* Michx.	Bluejack oak	*Q. incana* Bartr.
Bitternut hickory	*C. cordiformis* (Wangenh.) K. Koch	Turkey oak	*Q. laevis* Walt.
Pignut hickory	*C. glabra* (Mill.) Sweet	Laurel oak	*Q. laurifolia* Michx.
Pecan	*C. illinoensis* (Wangenh.) K. Koch	Overcup oak	*Q. lyrata* Walt.
Shellbark hickory	*C. laciniosa* (Michx. f.) Loud	Blackjack oak	*Q. marilandica* Muenchh.
Nutmeg hickory	*C. myristiciformis* (Michx. f.) Nutt.	Swamp chestnut oak	*Q. michauxii* Nutt.
Shagbark hickory	*C. ovata* (Mill.) K. Koch	Chinkapin oak	*Q. muehlenbergii* Engelm.
Mockernut hickory	*C. tomentosa* Nutt.	Water oak	*Q. nigra* L.
Allegheny chinkapin	*Castanea pumila* Mill.	Nuttall oak	*Q. nuttallii* Palmer
Chinkapin	*Castanopsis* (D. Don) Spach	Pin oak	*Q. palustris* Muenchh.
Catalpa	*Catalpa* spp. Scop.	Willow oak	*Q. phellos* L.
Sugarberry	*Celtis laevigata* Willd.	Chestnut oak	*Q. prinus* L.
Hackberry	*C. occidentalis* L.	Northern red oak	*Q. rubra* L.
Eastern redbud	*Cercis canadensis* L.	Shumard oak	*Q. shumardii* Buckl.
Flowering dogwood	*Cornus florida* L.	Post oak	*Q. stellata* Wangenh.
Hawthorn	*Crataegus* spp. L.	Black oak	*Q. velutina* Lam.
Common persimmon	*Diospyros virginiana* L.	Live oak	*Q. virginiana* Mill.
American beech	*Fagus grandifolia* Ehrh.	Black locust	*Robinia pseudoacacia* L.
White ash	*Fraxinus americana* L.	Willow	*Salix* spp. L.
Green ash	*F. pennsylvanica* Marsh.	Chinese tallowtree	*Sapium sebiferum* (L.) Roxb.
Water locust	*Gleditsia aquatica* Marsh.	Sassafras	*Sassafras albidum* (Nutt.) Nees
Honey locust	*G. triacanthus* L.	American basswood	*Tilia americana* L.
American holly	*Ilex opaca* Ait.	White basswood	*T. heterophylla* Vent.
Black walnut	*Juglans nigra* L.	Winged elm	*Ulmus alata* Michx.
Sweetgum	*Liquidambar styraciflua* L.	American elm	*U. americana* L.
Yellow-poplar	*Liriodendron tulipifera* L.	Cedar elm	*U. crassifolia* Nutt.
Osage-orange	*Maclura pomifera* (Raf.) Schneid.	Slippery elm	*U. rubra* Muhl.
Cucumbertree	*Magnolia acuminata* L.	Sparkleberry	*Vaccinium arboreum* Marsh.
Southern magnolia	*M. grandiflora* L.		

[a] Common and scientific names of tree species > 1.0 inch d.b.h. occurring in the FIA sample.

[b] Little (1979).

13

Appendix

Index of Tables

Table A.1—Output of industrial products by product and species group, Mississippi, 2007 and 2009

Table A.2—Roundwood receipts by product and species group, Mississippi, 2007 and 2009

Table A.3—Number of primary wood-using plants by type of mill, Mississippi, 1962 to 2009

Table A.4—Roundwood receipts by sawmill size, Mississippi, 2007 and 2009

Table A.5—Roundwood receipts by species and type of mill, Mississippi, 2009

Table A.6—Industrial roundwood movement by year and species group, Mississippi, 2007 and 2009

Table A.7—Industrial roundwood movement by product and species group, Mississippi, 2009

Table A.8—Saw-log volume by destination, source, and species group, Mississippi, 2009

Table A.9—Veneer volume by destination, source, and species group, Mississippi, 2009

Table A.10—Pulpwood volume by destination, source, and species group, Mississippi, 2009

Table A.11—Other industrial volume by destination, source, and species group, Mississippi, 2009

Table A.12—Primary mill residue volume by roundwood type, species group, and residue type, Mississippi, 2009

Table A.13—Disposal of residue at primary wood-using plants by product, species group, and type of residue, Mississippi, 2007 and 2009

Table A.14—Roundwood timber product output by county, product, and species group, Mississippi, 2009

Table A.15—Total roundwood output by product, species group, and source of material, Mississippi, 2009

Table A.16—Total roundwood output by species group, survey region, and ownership class, Mississippi, 2009

Table A.17—Total roundwood output by species group, detailed species group, and product, Mississippi, 2009

Table A.18—Total roundwood output by species group, detailed species group, and ownership class, Mississippi, 2009

Table A.1—Output of industrial products by product and species
group, Mississippi, 2007 and 2009

Product and species group	Year		Change	Change
	2007	2009		
	- - - - - - thousand cubic feet - - - - - -			percent
Saw logs				
Softwood	300,541	165,049	-135,492	-45.1
Hardwood	78,241	54,541	-23,700	-30.3
Total	378,782	219,590	-159,192	-42.0
Veneer logs				
Softwood	70,675	44,484	-26,191	-37.1
Hardwood	4,967	2,420	-2,547	-51.3
Total	75,642	46,904	-28,738	-38.0
Pulpwood[a]				
Softwood	274,250	298,486	24,236	8.8
Hardwood	126,305	97,936	-28,369	-22.5
Total	400,555	396,422	-4,133	-1.0
Composite panels				
Softwood	32,980	17,969	-15,011	-45.5
Hardwood	4,606	526	-4,080	-88.6
Total	37,586	18,495	-19,091	-50.8
Other industrial				
Softwood	1,534	3,433	1,899	123.8
Hardwood	0	195	195	—
Total	1,534	3,628	2,094	136.5
All industrial				
Softwood	679,980	529,421	-150,559	-22.1
Hardwood	214,119	155,618	-58,501	-27.3
Total	894,099	685,039	-209,060	-23.4

— = negligible.

[a] Includes roundwood delivered to nonpulpmills, then chipped and sold to
pulpmills (2,968,000 cubic feet in 2007 and 4,974,000 cubic feet in 2009).

Table A.2 — Roundwood receipts by product and species group, Mississippi, 2007 and 2009

Product and species group	Year			
	2007	2009	Change	Change
	- - - - - - thousand cubic feet - - - - - -			percent
Saw logs				
Softwood	307,267	162,096	-145,171	-47.2
Hardwood	77,637	53,233	-24,404	-31.4
Total	384,904	215,329	-169,575	-44.1
Veneer logs				
Softwood	79,504	48,085	-31,419	-39.5
Hardwood	4,116	2,363	-1,753	-42.6
Total	83,620	50,448	-33,172	-39.7
Pulpwood[a]				
Softwood	218,597	222,239	3,642	1.7
Hardwood	18,862	10,467	-8,395	-44.5
Total	237,459	232,706	-4,753	-2.0
Other industrial[b]				
Softwood	35,215	21,280	-13,935	-39.6
Hardwood	4,606	525	-4,081	-88.6
Total	39,821	21,805	-18,016	-45.2
Total output				
Softwood	640,583	453,700	-186,883	-29.2
Hardwood	105,221	66,588	-38,633	-36.7
Total	745,804	520,288	-225,516	-30.2

[a] Includes roundwood delivered to nonpulpmills, then chipped and sold to pulpmills (3,231,000 cubic feet in 2007 and 6,241,000 cubic feet in 2009).
[b] Includes 2,178,000 cubic feet used as industrial fuel in 2009.

Table A.3 — Number of primary wood-using plants by type of mill, Mississippi, 1962 to 2009

Type of mill	Year									
	1962	1966	1972	1976	1995	1999	2002	2005	2007	2009
	number									
Sawmills	290	305	241	218	84	84	92	93	66	57
Veneer mills	24	22	16	13	10	10	12	12	8	7
Pulpmills	6	7	8	7	7	7	6	5	5	5
Composite panel mills	0	0	0	0	2	2	3	3	2	2
Other mills	64	74	50	55	2	2	3	3	3	2
All plants	384	408	315	293	105	105	116	116	84	73

Table A.4—Roundwood receipts by sawmill size, Mississippi, 2007 and 2009

Sawmill size class[a]	2007			2009		
	Mills	Volume		Mills	Volume	
mmbf	number	mbf	percent	number	mbf	percent
< 1.0	0	0	0	2	1,410	0
1.0–4.99	8	23,069	1	10	30,620	3
5.0–9.99	16	121,784	6	13	89,875	7
10.0–49.99	26	568,574	26	24	532,008	44
> 50	16	1,427,924	67	8	549,024	46
Total	66	2,141,351	100	57	1,202,937	100

[a] Based on volume received as opposed to actual capacity.

Table A.5—Roundwood receipts by species and type of mill, Mississippi, 2009

			Type of mill			
			Veneer type			
Species	All mills	Sawmills	Pine plywood	Other veneer	Pulpmills[a]	Other mills[b]
			thousand cubic feet			
Softwood						
Yellow pine	230,132	160,767	48,085	0	NA	21,280
Eastern white pine	0	0	0	0	NA	0
Cedar	0	0	0	0	NA	0
Cypress	1,329	1,329	0	0	NA	0
Other softwood	0	0	0	0	NA	0
Unclassified	222,239	0	0	0	222,239	0
Total softwoods	453,700	162,096	48,085	0	222,239	21,280
Hardwood						
Blackgum and tupelo	223	223	0	0	NA	0
Soft maple	133	0	133	0	NA	0
Sweetgum	5,076	4,120	133	298	NA	525
Yellow-poplar	4,930	4,678	0	252	NA	0
Other soft hardwood	1,153	1,153	0	0	NA	0
Hickory	1,966	1,634	0	332	NA	0
Red oak	25,120	24,120	0	1,000	NA	0
White oak	9,108	8,959	0	149	NA	0
Other hard hardwood	8,412	8,346	0	66	NA	0
Unclassified	10,467	0	0	0	10,467	0
Total hardwoods	66,588	53,233	266	2,097	10,467	525
All species	520,288	215,329	48,351	2,097	232,706	21,805

NA = not applicable.

[a] Collected only by softwood and hardwood and includes roundwood chipped.

[b] Includes 2,178,000 cubic feet used as industrial fuel in 2009.

Table A.6—Industrial roundwood movement by year and species group, Mississippi, 2007 and 2009

Year	Production	Exported to other States	Retained	Imported from other States	Receipts
		thousand cubic feet			
		Softwood			
2007	679,980	116,344	563,636	76,947	640,583
2009	529,421	122,389	407,032	46,668	453,700
		Hardwood			
2007	214,119	120,462	93,657	11,564	105,221
2009	155,618	92,478	63,140	3,448	66,588
		All species			
2007	894,099	236,806	657,293	88,511	745,804
2009	685,039	214,867	470,172	50,116	520,288

Table A.7—Industrial roundwood movement by product and species group, Mississippi, 2009

Product and species group	Production	Exported to other States	Retained	Imported from other States	Receipts
		thousand cubic feet			
Saw logs					
Softwood	165,049	27,065	137,984	24,112	162,096
Hardwood	54,541	4,182	50,359	2,874	53,233
Total	219,590	31,247	188,343	26,986	215,329
Veneer logs					
Softwood	44,484	995	43,489	4,596	48,085
Hardwood	2,420	387	2,033	330	2,363
Total	46,904	1,382	45,522	4,926	50,448
Pulpwood[a]					
Softwood	298,486	93,740	204,746	17,493	222,239
Hardwood	97,936	87,713	10,223	244	10,467
Total	396,422	181,453	214,969	17,737	232,706
Other industrial[b]					
Softwood	21,402	589	20,813	467	21,280
Hardwood	721	196	525	0	525
Total	22,123	785	21,338	467	21,805
All products					
Softwood	529,421	122,389	407,032	46,668	453,700
Hardwood	155,618	92,478	63,140	3,448	66,588
Total	685,039	214,867	470,172	50,116	520,288

[a] Includes roundwood chipped.

[b] Includes composite panels, poles, posts, mulch, firewood, log homes, charcoal, and all other industrial mills.

Table A.8—Saw-log volume by destination, source, and species group, Mississippi, 2009

Destination and source	All species	Species group	
		Softwood	Hardwood
	thousand cubic feet		
Mississippi (retained)	188,343	137,984	50,359
Exports to:			
Alabama	16,566	13,996	2,570
Louisiana	13,566	13,038	528
Tennessee	1,115	31	1,084
Total	31,247	27,065	4,182
Imports from:			
Alabama	14,409	13,909	500
Louisiana	8,311	6,238	2,073
Tennessee	4,266	3,965	301
Total	26,986	24,112	2,874

Table A.10—Pulpwood volume by destination, source, and species group, Mississippi, 2009[a]

Destination and source	All species	Species group	
		Softwood	Hardwood
	thousand cubic feet		
Mississippi (retained)	214,969	204,746	10,223
Exports to:			
Alabama	57,679	20,902	36,777
Arkansas	16,237	992	15,245
Florida	1,645	1,645	0
Kentucky	7,703	20	7,683
Louisiana	66,480	42,232	24,248
Tennessee	31,430	27,949	3,481
Texas	279	0	279
Total	181,453	93,740	87,713
Imports from:			
Alabama	16,315	16,315	0
Louisiana	1,286	1,042	244
Tennessee	136	136	0
Total	17,737	17,493	244

[a] Includes roundwood delivered to nonpulpmills, then chipped and sold to pulpmills.

Table A.9—Veneer volume by destination, source, and species group, Mississippi, 2009

Destination and source	All species	Species group	
		Softwood	Hardwood
	thousand cubic feet		
Mississippi (retained)	45,522	43,489	2,033
Exports to:			
Alabama	387	0	387
Louisiana	995	995	0
Total	1,382	995	387
Imports from:			
Alabama	3,581	3,581	0
Louisiana	1,345	1,015	330
Total	4,926	4,596	330

Table A.11—Other industrial volume by destination, source, and species group, Mississippi, 2009[a]

Destination and source	All species	Species group	
		Softwood	Hardwood
	thousand cubic feet		
Mississippi (retained)	21,338	20,813	525
Exports to:			
Alabama	785	589	196
Total	785	589	196
Imports from:			
Alabama	76	76	0
Arkansas	391	391	0
Total	467	467	0

[a] Includes composite panels, poles, posts, mulch, firewood, log homes, charcoal, and all other industrial mills.

Table A.12—Primary mill residue volume by roundwood type, species group, and residue type, Mississippi, 2009

Roundwood type and species group	All types	Residue type			
		Bark	Coarse	Sawdust	Shavings
		thousand cubic feet			
Saw logs					
Softwood	99,456	14,364	47,258	23,906	13,928
Hardwood	29,590	6,082	11,929	11,169	410
Total	129,046	20,446	59,187	35,075	14,338
Veneer logs					
Softwood	29,436	4,561	12,444	12,431	0
Hardwood	1,697	279	698	720	0
Total	31,133	4,840	13,142	13,151	0
Pulpwood					
Softwood	22,332	22,332	0	0	0
Hardwood	1,285	1,285	0	0	0
Total	23,617	23,617	0	0	0
Other industrial[a]					
Softwood	2,074	1,983	91	0	0
Hardwood	65	65	0	0	0
Total	2,139	2,048	91	0	0
Total					
Softwood	153,298	43,240	59,793	36,337	13,928
Hardwood	32,637	7,711	12,627	11,889	410
Total	185,935	50,951	72,420	48,226	14,338

[a] Includes poles, pilings, posts, composite panels and other industrial products.

Table A.13—Disposal of residue at primary wood-using plants by product, species group, and type of residue, Mississippi, 2007 and 2009

Product and species group	All types		Bark		Coarse		Sawdust		Shavings	
	2007	2009	2007	2009	2007	2009	2007	2009	2007	2009
	thousand cubic feet									
Fiber products										
Softwood	99,111	53,116	0	0	99,111	53,116	0	0	0	0
Hardwood	17,927	11,232	0	0	17,927	11,232	0	0	0	0
Total	117,038	64,348	0	0	117,038	64,348	0	0	0	0
Particleboard										
Softwood	23,518	7,546	0	0	3,982	0	13,478	4,621	6,058	2,925
Hardwood	550	88	0	0	0	0	485	81	65	7
Total	24,068	7,634	0	0	3,982	0	13,963	4,702	6,123	2,932
Sawn products										
Softwood	883	23	0	0	883	23	0	0	0	0
Hardwood	208	187	0	0	208	187	0	0	0	0
Total	1,091	210	0	0	1,091	210	0	0	0	0
Industrial fuel										
Softwood	125,331	87,347	62,065	41,556	5,792	5,826	41,794	30,654	15,680	9,311
Hardwood	27,913	18,539	10,928	6,578	1,776	1,208	14,717	10,390	492	363
Total	153,244	105,886	72,993	48,134	7,568	7,034	56,511	41,044	16,172	9,674
Miscellaneous										
Softwood	16,531	5,266	4,332	1,684	413	828	9,809	1,062	1,977	1,692
Hardwood	4,221	2,463	1,802	1,133	297	0	1,922	1,290	200	40
Total	20,752	7,729	6,134	2,817	710	828	11,731	2,352	2,177	1,732
Not used										
Softwood	1,776	0	263	0	757	0	756	0	0	0
Hardwood	512	128	46	0	50	0	416	128	0	0
Total	2,288	128	309	0	807	0	1,172	128	0	0
All products										
Softwood	267,150	153,298	66,660	43,240	110,938	59,793	65,837	36,337	23,715	13,928
Hardwood	51,331	32,637	12,776	7,711	20,258	12,627	17,540	11,889	757	410
Total	318,481	185,935	79,436	50,951	131,196	72,420	83,377	48,226	24,472	14,338

Table A.14—Roundwood timber product output by county, product, and species group, Mississippi, 2009

County	All products		Saw logs		Veneer logs		Pulpwood[a]		Composite panels		Other industrial	
	Soft-wood	Hard-wood	Soft-wood	Hard-wood	Soft-wood	Hard-wood	Soft-wood	Hard-wood	Soft-wood	Hard-wood	Soft-wood	Hard-wood
					thousand cubic feet							
Adams	812	3,386	199	2,393	0	0	613	993	0	0	0	0
Alcorn	2,444	1,061	670	721	0	0	1,774	340	0	0	0	0
Amite	16,145	5,972	7,198	1,083	667	0	8,280	4,889	0	0	0	0
Attala	13,681	1,519	5,235	434	1,501	0	4,850	1,075	2,095	10	0	0
Benton	1,326	667	233	347	0	0	1,093	320	0	0	0	0
Bolivar	77	2,554	14	1,866	0	66	63	622	0	0	0	0
Calhoun	10,896	1,459	5,673	308	0	0	4,225	1,130	998	21	0	0
Carroll	2,467	1,663	479	263	0	0	921	1,299	1,047	101	20	0
Chickasaw	4,421	956	2,297	514	0	0	1,151	442	973	0	0	0
Choctaw	9,708	828	5,929	667	289	0	3,168	156	322	5	0	0
Claiborne	7,125	5,234	2,558	2,360	137	179	4,430	2,695	0	0	0	0
Clarke	14,992	2,324	5,317	156	1,795	205	7,846	1,963	0	0	34	0
Clay	3,002	1,202	943	840	0	0	1,464	362	595	0	0	0
Coahoma	16	2,314	16	1,944	0	0	0	370	0	0	0	0
Copiah	14,507	5,033	6,271	3,037	412	179	7,811	1,817	0	0	13	0
Covington	6,190	5,163	1,115	2,076	1,347	0	3,728	3,087	0	0	0	0
DeSoto	162	241	0	166	0	0	162	75	0	0	0	0
Forrest	3,521	815	120	285	948	0	2,435	530	0	0	18	0
Franklin	6,854	1,987	2,675	1,227	137	119	4,042	641	0	0	0	0
George	3,952	333	42	265	756	0	3,110	68	0	0	44	0
Greene	14,450	2,026	1,010	641	1,906	0	11,296	1,272	0	0	238	113
Grenada	3,475	525	1,577	189	0	0	1,224	283	644	53	30	0
Hancock	6,077	220	1,264	219	1,239	0	3,549	1	0	0	25	0
Harrison	3,206	263	656	263	676	0	1,842	0	0	0	32	0
Hinds	6,624	2,850	1,587	1,275	275	164	4,762	1,411	0	0	0	0
Holmes	3,557	3,909	396	1,122	0	0	2,597	2,686	564	101	0	0
Humphreys	144	229	144	132	0	0	0	97	0	0	0	0
Issaquena	0	1,398	0	624	0	0	0	774	0	0	0	0
Itawamba	6,123	5,344	3,114	1,368	0	0	1,918	3,976	1,091	0	0	0
Jackson	3,084	360	0	359	1,195	0	1,857	1	0	0	32	0
Jasper	11,455	944	2,988	53	3,729	0	4,725	891	0	0	13	0
Jefferson	5,678	2,481	1,518	1,749	0	0	4,148	732	0	0	12	0
Jefferson Davis	8,674	750	4,002	732	805	0	3,867	18	0	0	0	0
Jones	9,070	2,567	1,051	0	1,451	0	6,524	2,567	0	0	44	0
Kemper	20,468	2,704	9,713	179	1,333	92	8,319	2,433	0	0	1,103	0
Lafayette	6,113	1,046	2,091	576	0	0	3,024	465	998	5	0	0
Lamar	11,355	901	2,612	705	2,550	0	5,368	196	793	0	32	0
Lauderdale	22,625	5,756	10,154	319	1,192	90	11,237	5,347	0	0	42	0
Lawrence	16,549	455	7,412	291	687	0	8,450	164	0	0	0	0
Leake	9,654	1,109	2,823	647	1,239	0	5,351	462	241	0	0	0
Lee	1,756	369	386	145	0	0	378	224	992	0	0	0
Leflore	32	619	32	324	0	0	0	290	0	5	0	0
Lincoln	19,492	8,142	2,804	658	328	0	16,360	7,484	0	0	0	0
Lowndes	2,735	925	1,841	691	0	0	894	234	0	0	0	0

continued

Table A.14—Roundwood timber product output by county, product, and species group, Mississippi, 2009 (continued)

County	All products		Saw logs		Veneer logs		Pulpwood[a]		Composite panels		Other industrial	
	Soft-wood	Hard-wood	Soft-wood	Hard-wood	Soft-wood	Hard-wood	Soft-wood	Hard-wood	Soft-wood	Hard-wood	Soft-wood	Hard-wood
	thousand cubic feet											
Madison	5,888	1,270	608	471	398	0	4,799	794	80	5	3	0
Marion	18,909	4,305	4,250	493	1,107	0	13,019	3,812	496	0	37	0
Marshall	1,763	1,683	466	838	0	0	1,297	792	0	53 ·	0	0
Monroe	5,424	4,523	3,298	1,897	0	0	936	2,626	1,190	0	0	0
Montgomery	5,432	1,638	2,307	472	371	82	1,757	1,084	967	0	30	0
Neshoba	7,217	1,261	2,926	185	536	0	3,341	1,076	0	0	414	0
Newton	8,294	824	2,999	223	1,717	0	3,575	601	0	0	3	0
Noxubee	11,911	1,156	5,932	593	124	0	5,093	563	0	0	762	0
Oktibbeha	4,720	405	2,516	258	82	0	2,102	147	0	0	20	0
Panola	3,442	2,513	754	574	0	108	2,527	1,800	161	31	0	0
Pearl River	10,765	886	2,407	248	1,490	0	6,843	638	0	0	25	0
Perry	12,002	454	269	155	2,281	0	9,427	299	0	0	25	0
Pike	3,228	497	1,558	422	0	0	1,670	75	0	0	0	0
Pontotoc	2,974	832	988	79	0	82	796	671	1,190	0	0	0
Prentiss	2,465	1,105	349	610	0	0	1,521	495	595	0	0	0
Quitman	0	149	0	70	0	79	0	0	0	0	0	0
Rankin	10,540	1,031	2,306	532	1,526	104	6,708	395	0	0	0	0
Scott	5,306	4,387	1,021	520	549	0	3,736	3,867	0	0	0	0
Sharkey	106	458	106	193	0	0	0	265	0	0	0	0
Simpson	9,689	3,631	3,637	689	1,374	0	4,678	2,942	0	0	0	0
Smith	12,878	1,008	465	607	2,190	267	10,223	134	0	0	0	0
Stone	2,858	24	0	0	890	0	1,848	24	0	0	120	0
Sunflower	0	78	0	18	0	0	0	60	0	0	0	0
Tallahatchie	160	599	3	157	0	25	77	343	80	74	0	0
Tate	144	809	0	546	0	108	144	155	0	0	0	0
Tippah	3,953	2,091	586	427	0	0	3,367	1,664	0	0	0	0
Tishomingo	5,441	3,389	759	707	0	0	4,682	2,682	0	0	0	0
Tunica	0	167	0	134	0	0	0	33	0	0	0	0
Union	2,845	1,108	241	232	0	0	1,712	876	892	0	0	0
Walthall	4,764	875	878	863	338	0	3,516	12	0	0	32	0
Warren	689	3,961	295	2,281	0	247	394	1,433	0	0	0	0
Washington	0	1,440	0	949	0	0	0	491	0	0	0	0
Wayne	12,767	3,998	1,676	175	2,064	0	8,812	3,741	0	0	215	82
Webster	10,817	928	6,948	560	41	0	3,345	358	483	10	0	0
Wilkinson	7,128	3,777	1,694	1,568	0	0	5,434	2,209	0	0	0	0
Winston	13,882	4,849	4,484	550	812	0	8,506	4,299	80	0	0	0
Yalobusha	4,436	902	1,972	180	0	0	2,047	675	402	47	15	0
Yazoo	1,890	2,004	192	852	0	224	1,698	923	0	5	0	0
All counties	529,421	155,618	165,049	54,541	44,484	2,420	298,486	97,936	17,969	526	3,433	195

[a] Includes roundwood delivered to nonpulpmills, then chipped and sold to pulpmills (4,974,000 cubic feet in 2009).

Table A.15—Total roundwood output by product, species group, and source of material, Mississippi, 2009

Product and species group	All sources	Total	Growing-stock trees		Other sources
			Sawtimber	Poletimber	
			thousand cubic feet		
Saw logs					
Softwood	165,049	160,923	147,888	13,035	4,126
Hardwood	54,541	53,264	49,535	3,728	1,277
Total	219,590	214,186	197,423	16,763	5,404
Veneer logs and bolts					
Softwood	44,484	43,581	40,966	2,615	903
Hardwood	2,420	2,378	2,378	0	42
Total	46,904	45,959	43,344	2,615	945
Pulpwood					
Softwood	298,486	256,584	94,906	161,678	41,902
Hardwood	97,936	87,805	57,151	30,654	10,131
Total	396,422	344,389	152,057	192,332	52,033
Composite panels					
Softwood	17,969	16,172	8,066	8,106	1,797
Hardwood	526	482	270	211	44
Total	18,495	16,654	8,336	8,317	1,841
Poles and posts					
Softwood	890	854	820	34	36
Hardwood	0	0	0	0	0
Total	890	854	820	34	36
Other miscellaneous					
Softwood	2,543	1,279	959	320	1,264
Hardwood	195	191	143	48	4
Total	2,738	1,470	1,102	368	1,268
Total industrial products					
Softwood	529,421	479,392	293,605	185,787	50,029
Hardwood	155,618	144,119	109,478	34,641	11,499
Total	685,039	623,512	403,083	220,428	61,527
Residential fuelwood					
Softwood	3,061	2,399	1,587	812	662
Hardwood	14,799	13,829	9,241	4,587	970
Total	17,860	16,228	10,828	5,400	1,632
All products					
Softwood	532,482	481,792	295,192	186,599	50,690
Hardwood	170,417	157,948	118,719	39,229	12,469
Total	702,899	639,740	413,912	225,828	63,159

Numbers in rows and columns may not sum to totals due to rounding.

Table A.16—Total roundwood output by species group, survey region, and ownership class, Mississippi, 2009

Species group and survey region	Total	Ownership class		
		Public	Forest industry	Nonindustrial private
		thousand cubic feet		
Softwood				
Delta	6,710	0	163	6,547
North	109,109	2,985	21,216	84,908
Central	173,590	4,528	35,532	133,531
South	149,051	6,454	50,384	92,212
Southwest	94,022	4,571	17,723	71,728
Total softwoods	532,482	18,539	125,019	388,925
Hardwood				
Delta	21,771	607	4,145	17,019
North	41,845	496	4,664	36,685
Central	35,592	914	7,971	26,708
South	26,714	256	10,723	15,735
Southwest	44,495	1,762	8,070	34,663
Total hardwoods	170,417	4,035	35,573	130,809
All species	702,899	22,573	160,592	519,734

Numbers in rows and columns may not sum to totals due to rounding.

Table A.17—Total roundwood output by species group, detailed species group, and product, Mississippi, 2009

Species group and detailed species group	Total	Saw logs	Veneer logs	Pulpwood	Composite panels	Poles and posts	Other miscellaneous	Residential fuelwood
				thousand cubic feet				
Softwood								
Cedar	2,315	535	54	1,600	105	1	5	13
Longleaf-slash pine	58,717	9,367	10,031	38,092	488	271	130	338
Loblolly-shortleaf pine	456,614	150,951	32,812	249,953	17,275	600	2,399	2,624
Other yellow pines	13,594	4,105	1,461	7,826	101	14	8	78
Cypress	1,242	91	126	1,015	0	3	0	7
Total softwoods	532,482	165,049	44,484	298,486	17,969	890	2,543	3,061
Hardwood								
Soft maple	2,489	688	13	1,563	8	0	1	216
Hard maple	44	17	4	18	0	0	0	4
Other birch	704	269	0	360	14	0	0	61
Hickory	8,756	2,610	127	5,226	27	0	5	760
Beech	1,880	583	31	1,098	2	0	3	163
Ash	2,539	1,219	24	1,058	13	0	4	221
Black walnut	16	6	0	8	1	0	0	1
Sweetgum	28,430	8,744	383	16,731	92	0	11	2,469
Yellow-poplar	10,371	3,148	86	6,207	23	0	7	901
Blackgum-tupelo	6,758	1,922	49	4,148	16	0	36	587
Sycamore	3,038	1,718	35	1,014	6	0	0	264
Cottonwood	3,014	1,531	46	1,175	0	0	0	262
Black cherry	1,611	663	28	774	3	0	4	140
Select white oaks	15,615	4370	167	9641	60	0	22	1,355
Other white oaks	9,522	2725	120	5811	31	0	8	827
Select red oaks	12,023	4068	242	6623	42	0	4	1,044
Other red oaks	49,216	14889	801	29015	168	0	69	4,274
Basswood	231	74	6	130	1	0	0	20
Elm	4,096	1,547	52	2,123	13	0	5	356
Other eastern hardwoods	10,065	3,752	203	5,211	7	0	17	874
Total hardwoods	170,417	54,541	2,420	97,936	526	0	195	14,799
All species	702,899	219,590	46,904	396,422	18,495	890	2,738	17,860

Numbers in rows and columns may not sum to totals due to rounding.

Table A.18—Total roundwood output by species group, detailed species group, and ownership class, Mississippi, 2009

Species group and detailed species group	Total	Ownership class		
		Public	Forest industry	Nonindustrial private
		thousand cubic feet		
Softwood				
Cedar	2,315	40	182	2,093
Longleaf-slash pine	58,717	3,762	19,203	35,752
Loblolly-shortleaf pine	456,614	14,197	101,598	340,819
Other yellow pines	13,594	279	3,830	9,485
Cypress	1,242	260	206	776
Total softwoods	532,482	18,539	125,019	388,925
Hardwood				
Soft maple	2,489	50	496	1,944
Hard maple	44	0	1	43
Other birch	704	14	17	673
Hickory	8,756	149	1,661	6,946
Beech	1,880	36	457	1,387
Ash	2,539	55	968	1,515
Black walnut	16	5	1	10
Sweetgum	28,430	685	4,944	22,800
Yellow-poplar	10,371	155	2,278	7,938
Blackgum-tupelo	6,758	96	2,307	4,355
Sycamore	3,038	36	923	2,078
Cottonwood	3,014	98	489	2,426
Black cherry	1,611	51	285	1,276
Select white oaks	15,615	330	3,013	12,272
Other white oaks	9,522	262	1,878	7,382
Select red oaks	12,023	377	2,420	9,226
Other red oaks	49,216	1,278	9,900	38,035
Basswood	231	1	61	169
Elm	4,096	59	979	3,058
Other eastern hardwoods	10,065	296	2,495	7,273
Total hardwoods	170,417	4,035	35,573	130,809
All species	702,899	22,573	160,592	512,734

Numbers in rows and columns may not sum to totals due to rounding.